W9-BIK-681

English Paper Piecing

Fresh New Quilts from Bloom Creek  Vicki Bellino

Martingale
Create with Confidence

JUN 2013

Dedication

In loving memory of my dear, sweet friend, Anne Myers.

And to all of the wonderful friends I've made because of English paper piecing (EPP), especially to Pati Violick, who introduced me to EPP and without whom this book would never have come to be.

English Paper Piecing
Fresh New Quilts from Bloom Creek
© 2012 by Vicki Bellino

Martingale®
19021 120th Ave. NE, Suite 102
Bothell, WA 98011
ShopMartingale.com

No part of this product may be reproduced in any form, unless otherwise stated, in which case reproduction is limited to the use of the purchaser. The written instructions, photographs, designs, projects, and patterns are intended for the personal, noncommercial use of the retail purchaser and are under federal copyright laws; they are not to be reproduced by any electronic, mechanical, or other means, including informational storage or retrieval systems, for commercial use. Permission is granted to photocopy patterns for the personal use of the retail purchaser. Attention teachers: Martingale encourages you to use this book for teaching, subject to the restrictions stated above.

The information in this book is presented in good faith, but no warranty is given nor results guaranteed. Since Martingale has no control over choice of materials or procedures, the company assumes no responsibility for the use of this information.

Printed in China
17 16 15 14 13 12   8 7 6 5 4 3

Library of Congress Cataloging-in-Publication Data is available upon request.

ISBN: 978-1-60468-065-2

Credits

President & CEO • Tom Wierzbicki
Editor in Chief • Mary V. Green
Design Director • Paula Schlosser
Managing Editor • Karen Costello Soltys
Technical Editor • Ellen Pahl
Copy Editor • Melissa Bryan
Production Manager • Regina Girard
Cover & Text Designer • Regina Girard
Illustrator • Laurel Strand
Photographer • Brent Kane

Thanks to Konrad and Amy Moeller of Snohomish, Washington, for generously allowing us to photograph in their home.

Mission Statement

Dedicated to providing quality products and service to inspire creativity.

Contents

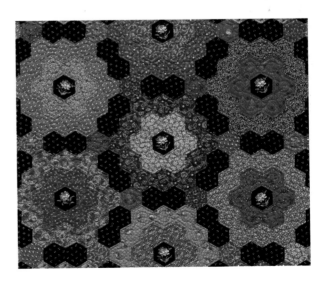

Introduction

*If you've never done English paper piecing,
I hope these projects will inspire you to
give it a try.*

For those of you who know me or are familiar with my pattern-design company, Bloom Creek, it will come as no surprise that I was thrilled when Martingale & Company asked me to write a book about English paper piecing! Ever since I was introduced to this wonderful technique about four years ago, I've tried to teach and share it with as many quilters as I possibly could. It's kind of like friendship bread . . . pay it forward and before you know it, we'll all be English paper piecing!

If it hadn't been for my good friend Pati Violick, who introduced me to English paper piecing, I most likely wouldn't be writing this book. She taught me this technique while we were traveling, as I had run out of hand work and was faced with a 12-hour road trip and nothing to keep me occupied. We went on our own little shop hop to look for a package of precut paper pieces. Pati provided me with fabric and a quick tutorial on the English-paper-piecing technique, and the rest is history! I think I basted more than 100 large diamonds on my trip home, and I haven't stopped since.

For those of you who are not very familiar with the technique of English paper piecing, you may think it involves only hexagons and Grandmother's Flower Garden quilts. It's so much more than that! This book will show you projects made with a variety of shapes, in a variety of ways. While I thoroughly enjoy English paper piecing, the reality is that I don't have the time to make many quilts that are completely pieced using this method. What I like to do is combine this technique with machine piecing and appliqué, as you'll discover in this book.

If you've never done English paper piecing, I hope these projects will inspire you to give it a try. There are so many things I like about this technique—it's very portable, makes great use of fabric scraps, and is extremely precise, to name a few. If you aren't a big fan of appliqué, try using this technique instead. I think you'll be amazed at the results!

English Paper Piecing 101

English paper piecing is a time-honored method of piecing, dating back to at least the early 1700s. Paper templates, cut to the exact finished size, are used as a guide to cut fabrics and as part of the construction process. The fabric is basted to the paper pieces, and the paper acts as a stabilizer, eliminating any stretching along bias edges. The paper remains in place until units are complete, guaranteeing that the pieces are the exact size and will fit together precisely.

As with many techniques used in quilting, there are several ways to do English paper piecing and a variety of supplies to choose from. The instructions that follow are for the method I prefer. For each project in this book, a pattern for cutting your own paper pieces is provided. However, I find that for a relatively small monetary investment, purchasing precut paper pieces is the way to go. It eliminates all of the tracing and cutting, and the paper pieces can be reused several times, giving you more bang for your buck. For all the patterns in this book, precut paper pieces are available at www.paperpieces.com. Most quilt shops also carry paper templates for English paper piecing. Note that the sizes given for the paper pieces in the materials lists refer to the length of the side of the shape. For example, a 1" hexagon measures 1" along each side.

Cutting

The cutting method is the same for all shapes. Place the paper shape onto the wrong side of your fabric and pin in place. Use scissors to cut out fabric a generous ¼" beyond the paper piece. An exact ¼" seam allowance isn't necessary.

For a speedier method, use a rotary cutter first to cut your fabric into squares or strips. Just make sure that these pieces are a generous ½" larger than the shape you're using. This makes final cutting much faster. You may have more fabric on the wrong side of the paper piece, but this won't show when the quilt is put together.

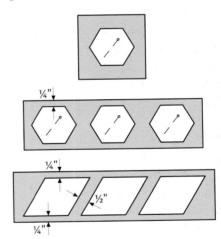

You can easily fussy cut your fabric by placing the paper template over the area in the print that you want to feature.

Making Your Own Paper Pieces

To make your own paper pieces, you'll need template plastic and a heavyweight paper. Trace the original pattern very carefully onto template plastic and cut it out to make an accurate master template. Trace around the master template onto the paper as many times as you need to, and carefully cut out each piece just inside the traced line. Your templates may be slightly less accurate than purchased die-cut pieces, but if you always use the master template for tracing, and cut carefully, they should work just fine.

Basting

After cutting, the seam allowances are folded over the paper templates and basted to the paper. This makes a precise finished-size shape, with no worries about that exact ¼" seam allowance. Each piece will be stabilized and ready to sew to other shapes.

1. Thread a size 8 or 9 Sharp needle with thread that contrasts with the fabric. This will make the basting much easier to see when you're ready to remove it. Knot the end.
2. Center the paper template over the fabric and pin in place.
3. Fold the seam allowance over the shape, and bring the needle up through the fabric and paper with the knot on the right side. Baste through the fabric and paper with long stitches.
4. Continue folding the fabric over the edges on all sides, basting through the fabric and paper with long stitches.
5. When you reach the point where you started, cut the thread, leaving about a 1" tail. It isn't necessary to tie a knot at the end of the basting.

Hexagons

The hexagon is the shape that probably comes to mind first when quilters think of English paper piecing. Hexagons are the basis of Grandmother's Flower Garden quilts, which were popular in the 1930s and '40s.

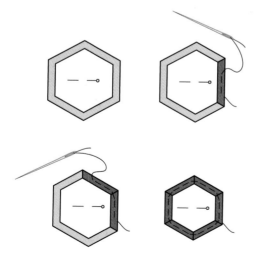

Diamonds

Diamonds may be my favorite shapes to work with using English paper piecing. They're so versatile. You can use them to create an entire quilt of diamonds, or make appliquéd stars and flowers. Note that in this book, I've used 60° diamonds exclusively (that is, diamonds with a 60° angle at each narrow point). When purchasing the precut diamonds, they're also called six-point diamonds because the stars they create when joined have six points.

When basting diamonds, it's easy to baste the wider angles by creating a small fold or pleat in the seam allowance. For the narrow points, think about where the sharp, angled points will be. If the points of your diamonds will not be on the outside, you can let your "tails wag." This means it is not necessary for you to fold the fabric over to a sharp point.

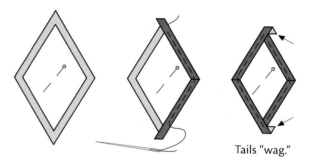

Tails "wag."

For a design such as a star or starflower, let the tails wag on the interior points, but fold over and baste a sharp point on the outer points. If you choose to hand appliqué your star to a background, you can let both tails wag and simply tuck under the outer tail with your appliqué needle.

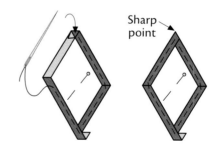

Sharp point

Curves

English paper piecing works well for curves too. When basting curved paper pieces, such as Dresden petals, start at the bottom edge of one long side and baste up the side to the curve. As you fold over the seam allowance around the curve, ease in the fullness and take smaller basting stitches. Baste circles in the same manner, beginning anywhere along the curve.

Dresdens and Chrysanthemums

These paper pieces are very similar, the only difference being that the ends of the Dresden pieces are rounded and the ends of the Chrysanthemum pieces are pointed. I use them together or on their own to create variations of the Dresden Plate.

When basting these pieces, it's not necessary to fold over and baste the short bottom end—just cut the fabric ⅛" to ¼" beyond the paper and leave a raw edge.

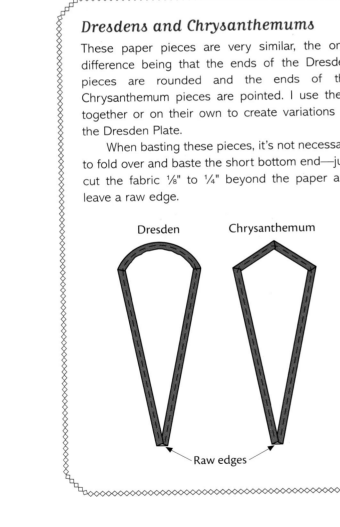

Dresden   Chrysanthemum

Raw edges

Whipstitching

Once you've basted your fabric to the paper pieces, it's time to whipstitch them together. This step is the same regardless of the paper shapes you're using. I've tried a variety of threads for this step, but ultimately I've found that a 40-weight machine-piecing thread or a 60-weight appliqué thread works best.

Hexagons

With right sides together and using thread to match or blend well with your fabric, take a small stitch just catching the folded edges of the fabric. When you reach the end of the piece, add the next paper piece and continue whipstitching.

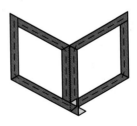

Diamonds

With right sides together, align two diamonds and whipstitch toward the center point. Once you reach the point of the tail, add the next diamond and whipstitch from the center tail to the outer edge.

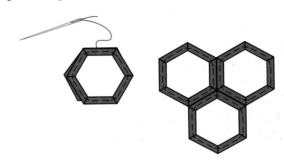

Dresdens and Chrysanthemums

With right sides together, align two Dresden or Chrysanthemum pieces. Begin at the bottom of one long side and whipstitch toward the curve or point. When you reach the beginning point of the curve or point, knot and cut the thread. Open up and whipstitch the next piece. Continue in this manner until the Dresden Plate is completed.

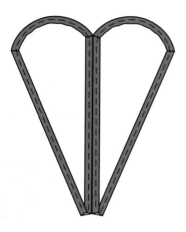

Finishing

If you're making a design such as a hexagon or diamond flower that will be appliquéd to a quilt block or other background, don't remove the basting and paper pieces until all of the paper pieces are whipstitched together. Then, press well on both sides, remove the basting thread, and pop out the paper pieces. Remember to save your paper pieces, as they can be reused several times.

Another option when appliquéing your English paper piecing to a block is to press well on both sides and remove the basting thread only. Then hand or machine appliqué the piece to the block. Cut away the fabric on the back under the appliqué, and then pop out the paper pieces. Try both ways to see which you prefer.

When making a quilt or other project that is almost entirely English paper pieced (such as "Just Judie" on page 49), don't remove the basting and the paper pieces until all sides have been whipstitched. Leave the basting and paper pieces in around the outer edges until the quilt center has been completed.

Quiltmaking Basics

The projects in this book use not only the English-paper-piecing technique, but also machine piecing and hand or machine appliqué. I'll share the techniques that work best for me, but if you prefer a different method to achieve the same result, use it! Regardless of what technique you choose, accuracy in cutting and piecing will give the best results. All of the piecing in this book is based on an accurate ¼" seam allowance unless otherwise indicated.

Freezer-Paper Appliqué

This method results in appliqué pieces with turned-under, finished edges. The pieces can be either hand or machine stitched in place on the block or quilt.

Preparing the Shapes

1. Trace the appliqué patterns onto the paper, non-shiny side of the freezer paper. For this method of appliqué, you'll need to cut a freezer-paper template for each piece needed. For example, if there are eight leaves in the quilt, you'll need to cut eight leaves out of freezer paper. Using scissors for cutting paper, cut out the shapes on the traced line.

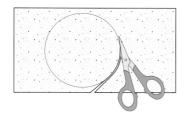

2. Iron the freezer-paper templates, shiny side down, onto the *right side* of the chosen appliqué fabric. Cut out each piece, adding a ¼" seam allowance around the entire shape.

Note: For small pieces or those with points, a slightly smaller seam allowance will work better.

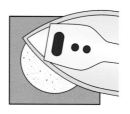 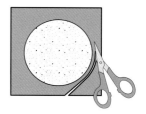

3. Carefully peel off the freezer-paper template. Turn the fabric piece over so that the wrong side is facing up. Center the freezer-paper template, shiny side facing up, on top of the fabric, with the ⅛" to ¼" seam allowance all around. Using a small iron and a smooth, firm surface, iron the seam allowance over the edge of the freezer-paper template.

4. On the wrong side of the shape, apply a few small dots of appliqué glue to the seam allowance and gently finger-press the shape into position on your block or quilt, leaving the freezer paper in place.

5. Stitch in place by hand or machine.

Stitching by Machine

To machine stitch the appliqué pieces in place, there are several options for both the thread and the stitch. If you don't want the thread to show, use a lightweight monofilament (clear for light fabrics and smoke for dark) and a 60/8 machine needle. Or, you can use a fine, lightweight thread that matches the color of the appliqué fabric and a 70/10 machine needle. Use an open-toe foot for good visibility and set your machine to a blind hem stitch, or a stitch similar to the one shown. This will result in a nearly invisible stitch. You can also use a small zigzag stitch, blanket stitch, or other decorative stitch if you want the stitching to be part of the design.

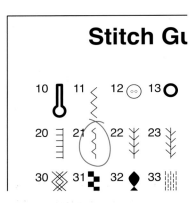

1. Begin stitching by using a straight stitch and take a few very short stitches to anchor the thread. Change to your chosen stitch and sew around the shape carefully, slowly turning the shape as you stitch around the curves. To pivot at corners and points, stop with the needle in the down position, lift the presser foot, and turn the appliqué piece. Do this when the needle is along the outer edge in the background fabric, not in the appliqué fabric. When you reach the starting point, change to a straight stitch and take a few short tacking stitches or backstitches to anchor the thread. Clip the threads and remove from the machine.

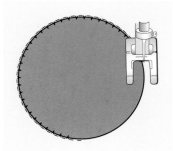

2. Turn the quilt or block over and cut away the fabric inside of the appliqué stitching, leaving a ¼" seam allowance. Remove the paper. Press the piece gently from the right side.

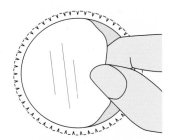

Stitching by Hand

Use an appliqué needle and thread that matches the appliqué fabric. Because the edges are already turned under, hand appliqué will be easy and relaxing.

1. Knot the thread and bring the needle up through the edge of the appliqué shape. Insert the needle into the background fabric right next to the appliqué and bring it up about 1/16" to 1/8" away, catching just a few threads along the folded edge of the appliqué shape. Continue around the shape until you reach the beginning stitch.

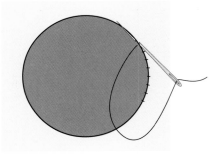

2. Knot the thread on the wrong side of the fabric and follow step 2 of "Stitching by Machine" to complete the block.

Fusible Appliqué

This method results in a raw edge, but one that's finished with machine stitching. There are many different fusible webs available on the market, but I find that a lightweight product works best. General instructions are provided here, but be sure to check the manufacturer's instructions beforehand for the product you use. This method is fast, but when tracing onto the fusible web, you'll need to reverse the patterns if they're not already reversed.

1. Trace the appliqué patterns onto the paper side of the fusible web.

2. Cut out the shapes approximately ¼" beyond the traced lines. For larger pieces, I use the "window-pane" technique and cut away the fusible web in the center, leaving approximately ¼" of web inside the traced line. This prevents stiffness and keeps the appliqués soft and flexible because they're not fused in the center.

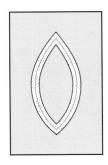

3. With the fusible side down and following the manufacturer's instructions, iron the fusible web onto the *wrong side* of the appliqué fabric. Cut out each piece on the traced lines.

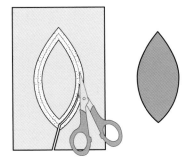

4. Remove the paper, position the appliqué pieces onto the block (or quilt), and iron in place, following the manufacturer's instructions. Machine stitch around the raw edges with a blanket stitch, satin stitch, or invisible stitch as described in "Stitching by Machine" on page 10.

Making Bias Vines

There are several different ways to make bias vines, but the following method is the one I find to be the easiest.

1. Open up the fabric so that it has no fold. Position the 45° line of an acrylic ruler on one selvage edge. Using a rotary cutter, cut along the long edge of the acrylic ruler. Move the ruler over to the desired width of the bias strip and make another cut. Continue in this manner until you've cut the required number of strips.

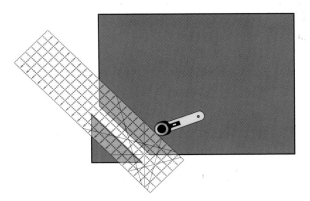

2. To make one long bias strip, sew strips together end to end at a 45° angle. Place strips right sides together, offsetting the ends by ¼". Sew, trim the points, and press the seam allowances open.

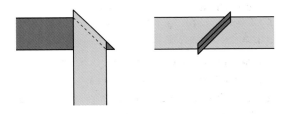

3. Fold the bias strip in half with *wrong sides* together and press. Sew ¼" from the raw edge along the entire length of the strip.

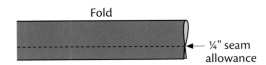

Fold

¼" seam allowance

4. Working on your ironing surface, insert a bias press bar (metal or plastic) into the bias strip and roll the seam allowance to the top when moving down the bias bar. Press well as you move the bias strip down the bar, pressing the seam allowances to the side. Continue until the entire strip has been pressed. (Spray sizing is helpful when pressing.) Remove the bias bar. ***Note:*** *If bias vines are narrow, you may need to trim the seam allowances to keep them from showing.*

Bias bar

5. Use dots of appliqué glue to position the vine on the quilt top. Appliqué by hand or machine using a blind stitch, blanket stitch, or small zigzag stitch.

Preparing for Machine Quilting

I machine quilt most of my own projects and will share the steps I use to prepare a quilt top for machine quilting. If you send your quilts out to be machine quilted, be sure to check with the quilter to determine how much larger than the quilt top the backing fabric and batting need to be.

1. Mark the quilting design onto the right side of the finished quilt top. Be sure to use a water-soluble marking pen or pencil. You can find an assortment of these at your local quilt shop.

2. Prepare the backing fabric. If your quilt is large, you'll have to piece the backing fabric together widthwise or lengthwise to obtain a piece approximately 4" larger than the quilt top. I press the seam allowances to one side.

3. Lay the backing fabric on a hard, flat surface (such as a table) with the wrong side facing up. Smooth the fabric out until it's completely smooth (but not stretched) and use tape or binder clips to fasten it to the table. Lay the batting on top, again smoothing it out but not stretching it. Lay the quilt on top of the batting with right side up, centering it on the batting and backing fabric.

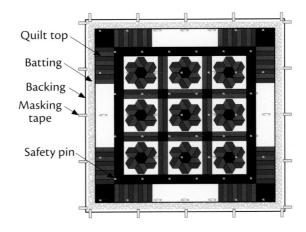

Quilt top
Batting
Backing
Masking tape
Safety pin

4. Pin through all layers with safety pins, spacing them approximately 4" apart over the entire quilt.

5. For machine quilting straight lines, or for stitching in the ditch, it's helpful to use a walking foot. For free-motion quilting, drop the feed dogs and attach the darning foot; this will allow you to quilt curved designs such as stippling or feathers.

6. When you've finished all of the machine quilting and removed the safety pins, spread the quilt out flat onto the floor and spray it with water to remove the water-soluble markings. Don't attempt to remove the markings in the washing machine before you sew on the binding!

7. After the quilt is dry, trim the batting and backing even with the quilt top and square up the corners.

Making a Hanging Sleeve

I recommend making a hanging sleeve for every project. It takes very little time and is much easier to sew onto the quilt as you're finishing it, rather than later on down the road. You never know when you might decide to enter your masterpiece into a quilt show or take it off of the bed and hang it on the wall.

1. Cut a 7"-wide strip of backing fabric the length of the top edge of the quilt, minus 2". Double fold a ½" hem at each end and stitch in place. Press in half lengthwise with wrong sides together, aligning the raw edges.

2. On the back of the quilt, center and align the raw edges of the sleeve along the top edge of the quilt. Pin or baste in place. After the binding is sewn to the quilt, whipstitch the folded edge of the sleeve to the backing fabric.

Binding the Quilt

All of the quilts in this book call for binding based on 2"-wide strips. For most projects, this narrow binding simply appeals to me. If you prefer a wider binding, however, feel free to cut your binding strips 2¼" or 2½" wide. Measure the entire perimeter of the quilt and add about 10". Divide this number by 40" to get the number of binding strips you'll need to cut for your quilt.

1. Sew together binding strips end to end at a 45° angle, trim, and press the seam allowances open. Cut one end of this long binding strip at a 45° angle, fold over ¼", and press. Fold the long binding strip in half lengthwise, wrong sides together, and press.

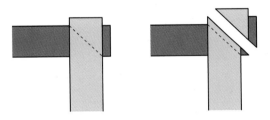

2. Align the raw edges of the binding strip with the raw edges of the quilt top, beginning with the 45° end of the binding strip. Using a ¼" seam allowance, begin sewing approximately 4" from the end of the binding strip and continue until you're ¼" from the corner. Stop stitching and remove the quilt from the machine.

4"

Quilt top

3. Fold the binding up as shown to create a 45° angle. Then fold the binding down to align the raw edges with the next side of the quilt. Begin sewing at the fold and continue to the next corner. Repeat the mitering process at each corner.

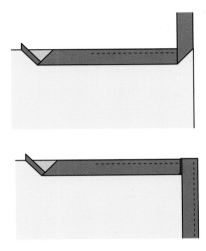

4. When you're nearing the binding tail where you started, trim the binding strip at a 45° angle so that the end of the binding will overlap the beginning of the binding by 2". Tuck the newly trimmed end into the turned-under end, align the raw edges, and continue sewing until you've stitched over the first few stitches.

5. Turn the folded edge of the binding over the seam allowance to the back of the quilt and stitch in place by hand.

Suitable for Framing

I often find that beautiful fabrics lend themselves to a simple quilt design, which was the case with this two-color quilt. By simply framing the lovely floral print with appliquéd hexagon blocks made from assorted red fabrics, the quilt comes together nicely without any other pieced blocks or borders. To complete the quilt, I added a simple appliquéd chain and small hexagon flowers to enhance the romantic feeling. Freezer paper and machine appliqué for the oval chains make quick work of the border.

Materials

Yardage is based on 42"-wide fabric. Note that the narrow red strips in the quilt are referred to as "frames" and the wider strips are "borders."

3¼ yards of small-scale white-and-red print #1 for blocks, large and small hexagons, border 1, and border 5

1¾ yards of large-scale white-and-red floral print for center rectangle, border 2, and border 4

1⅓ yards of small-scale white-and-red print #2 for blocks and large and small hexagons

1¾ yards of red print #1 for hexagons, third and fifth frames, and binding

1⅛ yards of red print #2 for hexagons and second and fourth frames

1½ yards of red print #3 for hexagons and appliquéd oval rings

1½ yards of red print #4 for hexagons, first frame, and appliquéd oval rings

5 yards of fabric for backing

77" x 88" piece of batting

98 paper hexagons, 2"

126 paper hexagons, 1"

Size 8 or 9 Sharp needle and thread to match fabric

Freezer paper, pencil, appliqué glue, monofilament (or appliqué thread to match fabric)

OR 2¼ yards of lightweight, 18"-wide fusible web for the fusible-appliqué method

Cutting

Refer to "English Paper Piecing 101" on page 5 for cutting hexagons; baste all hexagons to the papers. Refer to "Freezer-Paper Appliqué" on page 9 or "Fusible Appliqué" on page 10 for cutting and preparing oval rings for appliqué. Patterns are on pages 20 and 21.

From small-scale white-and-red print #1, cut:
- 7 squares, 11½" x 11½"
- 8 strips, 7½" x 42"
- 2 strips, 2½" x 42"; crosscut into:
  2 pieces, 2½" x 23½"
  2 pieces, 2½" x 8½"
- 7 large hexagons and 10 small hexagons

From small-scale white-and-red print #2, cut:
- 7 squares, 11½" x 11½"
- 7 large hexagons and 8 small hexagons

From red print #1, cut:
- 3 strips, 1½" x 42"; crosscut into:
  2 pieces, 1½" x 20½"
  2 pieces, 1½" x 33½"
- 7 strips, 1½" x 42
- 18 large hexagons and 24 small hexagons
- 8 binding strips, 2" x 42"

From red print #2, cut:
- 3 strips, 1½" x 42"; crosscut into:
  2 pieces, 1½" x 25½"
  2 pieces, 1½" x 12½"
- 6 strips, 1½" x 42"
- 24 large hexagons and 24 small hexagons

Continued on page 17

Quilted by Vicki Bellino
Finished Quilt: 72½" x 83½"
Finished Block: 11" x 11"

From red print #3, cut:
- 24 large hexagons and 24 small hexagons
- 4 A oval rings and 4 B oval rings

From red print #4, cut:
- 2 strips, 1½" x 42"; crosscut into:
  2 pieces, 1½" x 19½"
  2 pieces, 1½" x 6½"
- 18 large hexagons and 36 small hexagons
- 4 A oval rings and 2 B oval rings

From the large-scale white-and-red floral, cut:
- 1 rectangle, 6½" x 17½"
- 6 strips, 5½" x 42"
- 3 strips, 3½" x 42"; crosscut into:
  2 pieces, 3½" x 14½"
  2 pieces, 3½" x 31½"

Making the Hexagon Blocks

1. Whipstitch together the large hexagons using six of the same red print and one small-scale white-and-red print #1 for the center to make a hexagon flower. (Refer to "English Paper Piecing 101" on page 5 as needed.) Repeat to make seven of these hexagon flowers. These are block A. Make seven using the small-scale white-and-red print #2 for the center; these are block B. Press the hexagon flowers well on both sides, remove the basting thread, and gently pop out the paper pieces.

2. Center each of the block A hexagon flowers onto an 11½" white-and-red print #1 square. Apply a few drops of appliqué glue around the wrong side of the hexagon flower near the outer edge and finger-press in place. Machine or hand appliqué around each hexagon flower. Repeat to appliqué the block B hexagon flowers onto the 11½" white-and-red print #2 squares.

Block A.
Make 7.

Block B.
Make 7.

3. Whipstitch together the small hexagons in the same manner as the large hexagons to make 18 hexagon flowers. These will be used in the outer border.

Quilt-Top Assembly

Refer to the assembly diagrams and press all seam allowances toward the newly added frame or border as you go.

1. Stitch 1½" x 6½" red print #4 strips to the top and bottom of the 6½" x 17½" large-scale white floral rectangle. Stitch a 1½" x 19½" red print #4 strip to each side.

2. Stitch 2½" x 8½" white-and-red print #1 strips to the top and bottom of the quilt center, and then add a 2½" x 23½" strip to each side.

3. Repeat step 1 with the 1½" x 12½" red print #2 strips and the 1½" x 25½" red print #2 strips.

4. Repeat steps 2 and 3 with the 3½" x 14½" and 3½" x 31½" large-scale white floral strips, followed by the 1½" x 20½" and 1½" x 33½" red print #1 strips.

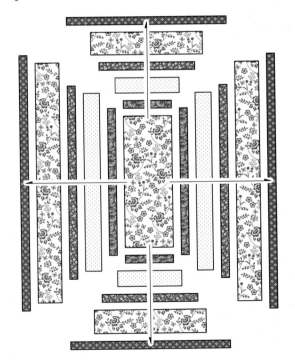

5. Alternating block A and block B and rotating every other block a quarter-turn, make block rows as shown. Press in the direction of the arrows. Sew the rows to the quilt and press.

6. Sew together the remaining 1½" x 42" red print #2 strips end to end. From this long strip, cut two pieces 44½" long and two pieces 57½" long. Sew the 44½"-long pieces to the top and bottom of the quilt, and then add the 57½"-long strips to each side.

7. Repeat step 6 with the 5½"-wide large-scale white floral strips; cut top and bottom strips 46½" long and side strips 67½" long.

8. Repeat step 6 with the 1½"-wide red print #1 strips, cutting top and bottom strips 56½" long and side strips 69½" long.

9. For the outer border, sew together the 7½"-wide white-and-red print #1 strips end to end. Cut two pieces 58½" long for the top and bottom borders and two pieces 83½" long for each side. (Measure your quilt first and adjust border lengths as needed.)

10. Glue baste two A oval rings, one B oval ring, and two small hexagon flowers in place on both the top and bottom border strips using the diagram as a placement guide. Machine or hand appliqué in place. Sew these border strips to the top and bottom edges of the quilt.

11. On each side border, appliqué two A oval rings, two B oval rings, and three small hexagon flowers in place. Sew to the sides of the quilt.

12. Glue baste, and then appliqué two small hexagon flowers in place on each corner as shown to link the oval rings.

Finishing

Refer to page 12 for details on marking, layering, basting, and quilting your project. Then use the 2"-wide red print #1 strips to bind the quilt.

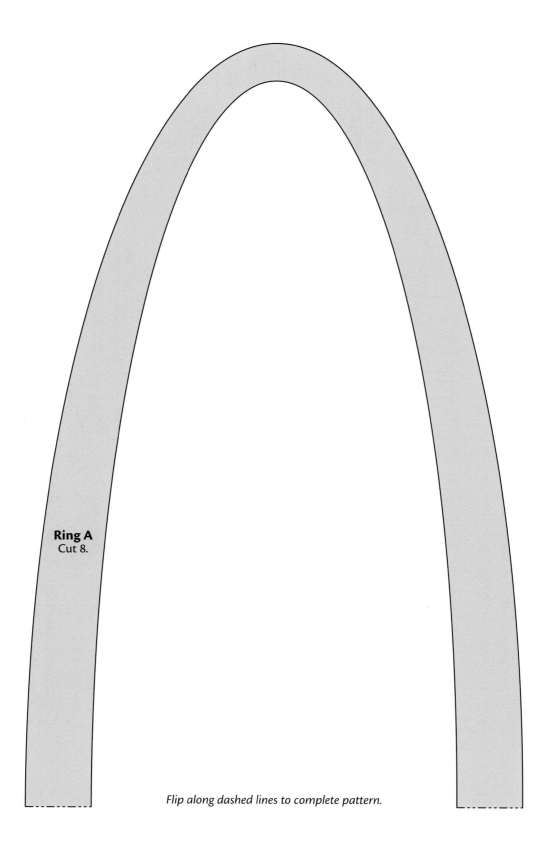

Ring A
Cut 8.

Flip along dashed lines to complete pattern.

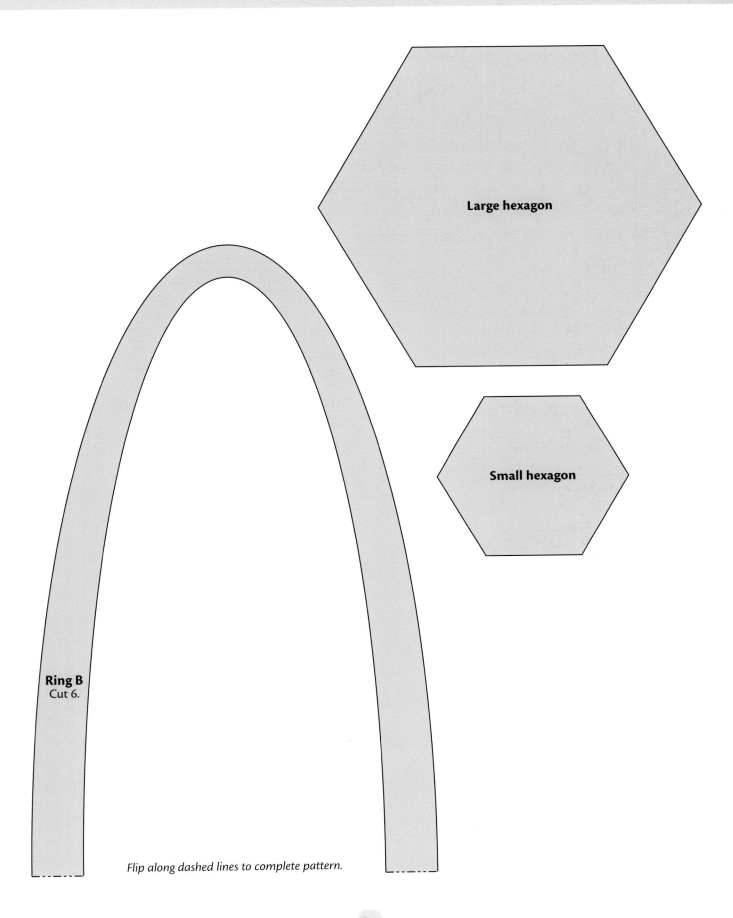

Large hexagon

Small hexagon

Ring B
Cut 6.

Flip along dashed lines to complete pattern.

Black and Red and Gold All Over

This quilt is my spin on the traditional Grandmother's Flower Garden. It's also a great project for digging into your stash, as each flower uses just a small amount of fabric. As you'll often find with English paper piecing, fussy cutting a design or flower from your fabric can add a great touch. You'll start looking a little more closely at the designs in fabric before you begin a project using English paper piecing!

Materials

Yardage is based on 42"-wide fabric.

1 yard of black floral print for hexagon flower centers, outer border, and binding

½ yard of black print for joining hexagons

¼ yard of gold-and-cream striped fabric for inner border

1 fat eighth *each* of 10 assorted red prints for hexagon flowers

1 fat eighth *each* of 8 assorted gold prints for hexagons

2⅓ yards of fabric for backing

42" x 45" piece of batting

351 paper hexagons, 1"

Size 8 or 9 Sharp needle and thread to match fabric

Cutting

Refer to "English Paper Piecing 101" on page 5 for cutting hexagons; baste all hexagons to the papers. The hexagon pattern is on page 26.

From the assorted red prints, cut *a total of:*
- 104 hexagons*

From the assorted gold prints, cut *a total of:*
- 154 hexagons**

From the black floral print, cut:
- 4 strips, 4½" x 42"
- 5 strips, 2" x 42"
- 17 hexagons

From the black print, cut:
- 76 hexagons

From the gold-and-cream striped fabric, cut:
- 4 strips, 1" x 42"

*Cut 7 sets of 6 matching hexagons, 4 sets of 4 matching hexagons, and 6 sets of 3 matching hexagons.

**Cut 7 sets of 12 matching hexagons and 10 sets of 7 matching hexagons.

Quilted by Veronica Nurmi
Finished Quilt: 41" x 37½"

Making the Hexagon Flowers

1. Whipstitch together six hexagons of the same red print and one hexagon of the black floral print. Whipstitch 12 gold hexagons of the same print around this flower. Make seven using the assorted red and gold prints. (The basting and papers from the red and black hexagons may be removed at this point.)

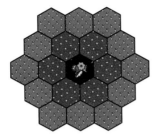

Make 7.

2. Make four partial hexagon flowers following step 1, using four hexagons of the same red print, one hexagon of the black floral print, and seven hexagons of the same gold print. These will be used at the top and bottom of the quilt.

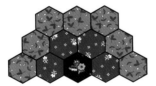

Make 4.

3. Make six additional partial hexagon flowers using three hexagons of the same red print, one hexagon of the black floral print, and seven hexagons of the same gold print. These will be used on each side of the quilt.

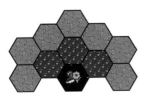

Make 6.

Quilt-Top Assembly

1. Whipstitch the black print and assorted red connector hexagons to the flower blocks until all hexagons have been used, forming the quilt center.

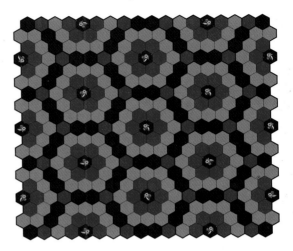

2. Trim the top and bottom of the quilt, followed by the sides.

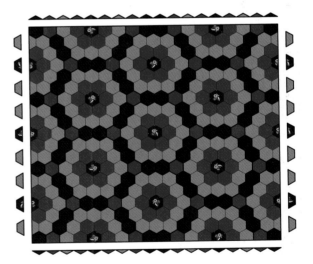

3. Measure the sides of the quilt and cut gold-and-cream striped inner-border strips to fit. Sew a border strip to each side of the quilt. Repeat for the top and bottom.

4. Repeat step 3 using the 4½"-wide strips of black floral print.

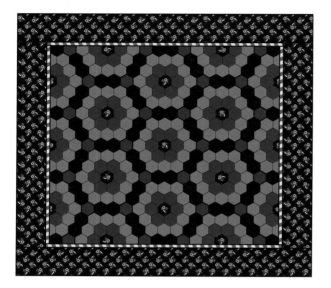

Finishing

Refer to page 12 for details on marking, layering, basting, and quilting your project. Then use the 2"-wide black floral-print strips to bind the quilt.

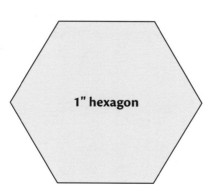

1" hexagon

Spinagons

When you look at the hexagon blocks in this quilt, you may think they're made up of half-hexagon pieces. Surprise! They're actually prepared with a timesaving strip-set method, thus eliminating half of the work. By careful placement of the two-color hexagons, you'll see a spinning effect appear before your eyes! This would be a great project for precut 2½"-wide strips.

Materials

Yardage is based on 42"-wide fabric.

1¼ yards of black print #1 for hexagon blocks, inner border, and binding

⅝ yard *each* of 4 assorted light prints for hexagon blocks and outer border

½ yard *each* of 4 assorted red prints for hexagon blocks, sashing, and outer border

½ yard *each* of 4 assorted blue prints for hexagon blocks, sashing, and outer border

½ yard of black print #2 for corner squares and hexagon blocks

3½ yards of fabric for backing

62" x 62" piece of batting

Size 8 or 9 Sharp needle and thread to match fabric

63 paper hexagons, 2"

Appliqué glue

Cutting

Refer to "English Paper Piecing 101" on page 5 for cutting hexagons; baste all hexagons to the papers. The hexagon pattern is on page 32.

From *each* of the assorted red and blue prints, cut:
- 2 strips, 2½" x 42" (16 total)
- 1 strip, 2" x 42" (8 total)
- 8 rectangles, 2" x 6½" (64 total)

From black print #1, cut:
- 5 strips, 3½" x 42"
- 6 strips, 2" x 42"
- 4 hexagons

From black print #2, cut:
- 4 squares, 6½" x 6½"
- 4 squares, 3½" x 3½"
- 5 hexagons

From the assorted light prints, cut *a total of*:
- 9 squares, 11½" x 11½" (2 each of 3 prints and 3 of the fourth print)
- 4 rectangles, 6½" x 21½" (1 of each light print)

Making the Hexagon Blocks

1. With right sides together, stitch a 2½"-wide blue strip to a 2½"-wide red strip. Press the seam allowances open. Make eight of these strip sets.

2. Place the paper hexagons on the strip sets, aligning the center points of the hexagons with the strip-set seams. Cut a total of 54 hexagons (six from each strip set and an additional hexagon from each of six strip sets). Be sure to add ¼" all around for seam allowances. Eight of the blocks will each use six hexagons from the same strip set; the center block will use a variety. Baste the fabric hexagons to the paper hexagons, referring to "English Paper Piecing 101" on page 6 for basting instructions.

3. Whipstitch together six matching red/blue hexagons and one black print #1 hexagon, noting the orientation of the red and blue prints as you add each hexagon. Make four. Repeat this step using a black print #2 hexagon in the center and reversing the position of the red and blue prints. Make four. Press well on both sides, remove the basting, and pop out the paper pieces.

Make 4.

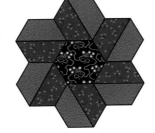
Make 4.

4. For the center hexagon block, whipstitch six assorted hexagons to a black print #2 hexagon so that the blue is next to the center hexagon. Press well on both sides, remove the basting, and pop out the paper pieces.

5. Center each of the hexagons from steps 3 and 4 onto an 11½" light-print square and glue baste in place. Hand or machine appliqué to the block. Make nine blocks as shown.

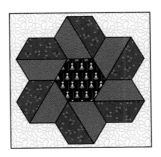
Make 4.

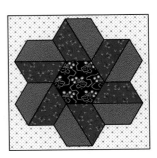
Make 4.

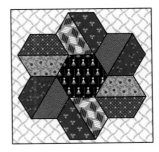
Make 1.

Assembly

1. With right sides together, make four red/blue strip sets using the 2" x 42" strips. Press toward the blue print. Crosscut three segments, 11½" wide, from each strip set to make a total of 12 sashing units, 3½" x 11½".

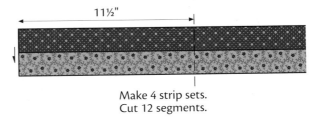

11½"

Make 4 strip sets.
Cut 12 segments.

Quilted by Vicki Bellino
Finished Quilt: 57½" x 57½"
Finished Block: 11" x 11"

2. Arrange the hexagon blocks, sashing units, and 3½" black print #2 squares in rows, referring to the photo at left for block placement. Sew the pieces in each row together and press toward the sashing units. Sew the rows together; press.

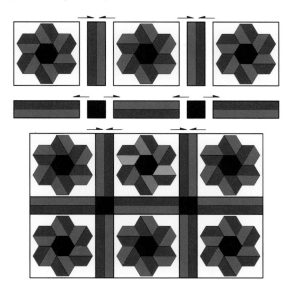

Adding the Borders

1. Crosscut two of the 3½"-wide black print #1 strips to 39½" long and sew them to the top and bottom of the quilt. Sew the remaining three strips together and cut two pieces 45½" long. Sew one to each side of the quilt.

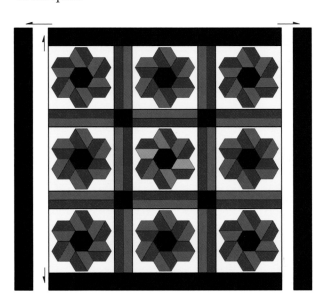

2. Sew together eight assorted red and blue 2" x 6½" rectangles, alternating the colors to create a piano-key border unit measuring 6½" x 12½". Make eight.

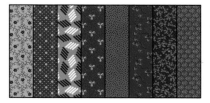

Make 8.

3. Sew a unit from step 2 to each end of the 6½" x 21½" light-print strips. Make four. Sew one of these strips each to the top and bottom edges of the quilt. Sew a 6½" black print #2 square to each end of the remaining two border strips and sew to each side of the quilt.

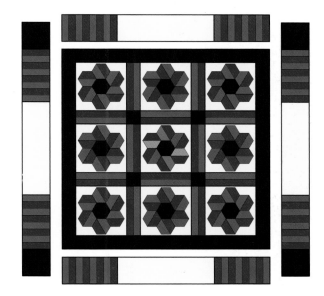

Finishing

Refer to page 12 for details on marking, layering, basting, and quilting your project. Then use the 2"-wide black print #1 strips to bind the quilt.

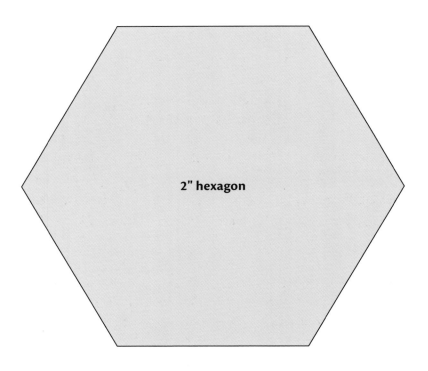

2" hexagon

Starflowers

Finished Quilt: 11½" x 14½"
Finished Block: 4" x 4"

While this particular project would make a great little wall hanging or table topper, I thought it would look delightful displayed in a frame. I bought a rustic-looking ready-made frame and had it framed by a professional, but you could certainly frame this yourself if you wish. The measurements given fit a frame with a standard 11" x 14" opening.

Materials

1 fat quarter *each of 2* assorted cream-and-black prints for large and small circles and border

1 fat eighth *each of 4* assorted small-scale black prints for blocks and starflowers

14" x 17" piece of batting

36 paper 6-point diamonds, 1"

Size 8 or 9 Sharp needles and thread to match fabric

Freezer paper, appliqué glue, monofilament thread (or thread to match fabric)

OR 12" x 18" piece of lightweight fusible web for the fusible appliqué method

Picture frame with 11" x 14" opening

Note: *For the framed piece, you will not need backing or binding fabric. If you choose to make a small quilt, you'll need ⅝ yard of fabric, which is enough for both backing and binding.*

Cutting

Refer to "English Paper Piecing 101" on page 5 for cutting diamonds; baste all diamonds to the papers. Baste the circles to papers or refer to "Freezer-Paper Appliqué" on page 9. Patterns are on page 36.

From cream-and-black print #1, cut:
- 3 large circles and 3 small circles
- 2 strips, 2" x 14½"

From cream-and-black print #2, cut:
- 3 large circles and 3 small circles
- 2 strips, 1½" x 8½"

From the assorted small black prints, cut *a total of:*
- 6 squares, 5" x 5"
- 36 diamonds

Making the Starflower Blocks

1. Whipstitch together six assorted diamonds to form a starflower. Press well and remove basting thread. Make six starflowers.

Make 6.

2. Center a large cream-and-black print circle onto each of the assorted 5" black print squares. Appliqué in place.

Make 6.

3. Square up the blocks to 4½" x 4½".
4. Remove paper pieces from each starflower, center onto the blocks, and glue baste in place. Hand or machine appliqué to the blocks. Center a small cream-and-black circle onto each starflower and appliqué in place.

Make 6.

Assembly

1. Arrange the starflower blocks to your liking and sew together, pressing seam allowances in the direction of the arrows in the diagram.

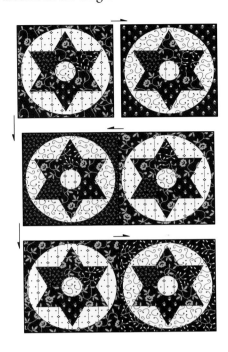

2. Sew the 1½" x 8½" cream print #2 strips to the top and bottom of the quilt, pressing toward the border. Sew a 2" x 14½" cream print #1 strip to each side and press.

Finishing

For framing, lay the completed quilt top onto the piece of batting and pin or baste together. Hand or machine quilt as desired. If you've chosen to make a small quilt, refer to page 12 for details on marking, layering, basting, quilting, and binding your project.

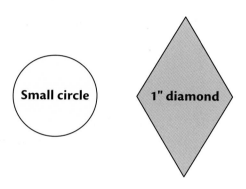

Small circle

1" diamond

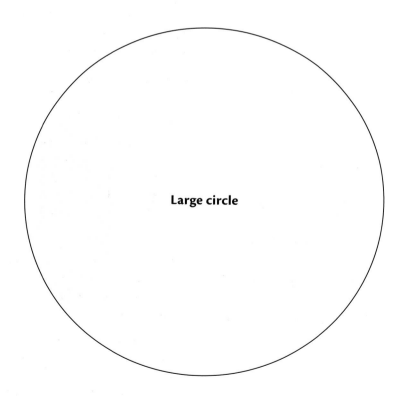

Large circle

Cabin Flowers

I think my favorite shape for English paper piecing is the diamond. Diamonds can be joined to create such stunning designs, such as the starflower in this quilt. I enjoy combining English paper piecing with machine piecing and appliqué, which is what I did in this project. I wanted to combine Starflower blocks with the very first quilt block I ever made—the Log Cabin block. One thing led to another, and the result is this queen-size version of my Cabin Flowers table-topper pattern (available on my website).

Materials

Yardage is based on 42"-wide fabric.

1 yard of cream print #1 for Log Cabin blocks and Starflower blocks

1 yard of cream print #2 for Log Cabin blocks and Starflower blocks

⅔ yard of blue print #1 for Log Cabin blocks and appliqués

1 yard of blue print #2 for Log Cabin blocks and appliqués

1¼ yards of blue print #3 for Log Cabin blocks and appliqués

⅔ yard of blue print #4 for Log Cabin blocks and appliqués

1 yard of blue print #5 for Log Cabin blocks and appliqués

1¼ yards of blue print #6 for Log Cabin blocks and appliqués

½ yard of light-brown print #1 for Log Cabin blocks and appliqués

⅝ yard of light-brown print #2 for Log Cabin blocks and appliqués

⅞ yard of brown print #1 for Log Cabin blocks and appliqués

1 yard of brown print #2 for Log Cabin blocks and appliqués

⅞ yard of brown print #3 for Log Cabin blocks and appliqués

1 yard of brown print #4 for Log Cabin blocks and appliqués

¾ yard of brown print for binding

8 yards of fabric for backing

94" x 94" piece of batting

160 paper 6-point diamonds, 1½"

Size 8 or 9 Sharp needle and thread to match fabric

Appliqué glue

Cutting

Refer to "English Paper Piecing 101" on page 5 for cutting diamonds; baste all diamonds to the papers. Baste the circles to papers or refer to "Freezer-Paper Appliqué" on page 9. Patterns are on page 42.

From *each* of cream prints #1 and #2, cut:
- 10 squares, 9¼" x 9¼"
- 40 squares, 1¾" x 1¾"

From *each* of light-brown prints #1 and #2, cut:
- 5 strips, 1¾" x 42"; crosscut 40 squares, 1¾" x 1¾" and 40 pieces, 1¾" x 3"
- 10 diamonds
- 10 circle A and 10 circle B (light-brown print #2 only)

From *each* of blue prints #1 and #4, cut:
- 8 strips, 1¾" x 42"; crosscut 40 pieces, 1¾" x 3" and 40 pieces, 1¾" x 4¼"
- 20 diamonds

From *each* of brown prints #1 and #3, cut:
- 11 strips, 1¾" x 42"; crosscut 40 pieces, 1¾" x 4¼" and 40 pieces, 1¾" x 5½"
- 10 diamonds (brown print #1 only)
- 10 circle A and 10 circle B (brown print #3 only)

Continued on page 39

From *each* of blue prints #2 and #5, cut:
- 14 strips, 1¾" x 42"; crosscut into:
  40 pieces, 1¾" x 5½"
  40 pieces, 1¾" x 6¾"
- 20 diamonds

From *each* of brown prints #2 and #4, cut:
- 16 strips, 1¾" x 42"; crosscut into:
  40 pieces, 1¾" x 6¾"
  40 pieces, 1¾" x 8"
- 5 circle B and 20 stems (brown print #2 only)
- 10 diamonds (brown print #4 only)

From *each* of blue prints #3 and #6, cut:
- 18 strips, 1¾" x 42"; crosscut into:
  40 pieces, 1¾" x 8"
  40 pieces, 1¾" x 9¼"
- 20 diamonds
- 5 circle C (blue print #6 only)

From the brown print for binding, cut:
- 9 strips, 2" x 42"

Making the Log Cabin Blocks

You'll make 80 Log Cabin blocks, 40 each of two different fabric combinations. Follow the steps and diagrams below and press the seam allowances toward the piece just added.

1. Sew a 1¾" cream print #1 square and a 1¾" light-brown print #1 square together as shown. Add a 1¾" x 3" light-brown rectangle, followed by a 1¾" x 3" blue print #1 rectangle and a 1¾" x 4¼" blue print #1 rectangle. Continue to add rectangles of brown print #1, blue print #2, brown print #2, and blue print #3. The block should measure 9¼" x 9¼". Make 40.

Make 40.

2. Repeat step 1 using cream print #2, light-brown print #2, blue print #4, brown print #3, blue print #5, brown print #4, and blue print #6. Make 40.

Make 40.

Making the Starflower Blocks

1. Whipstitch together one each of six assorted blue diamonds to form a starflower. Press well on both sides, remove the basting thread, and pop out the paper pieces. Make 20.

Make 20.

2. Fold a 9¼" cream print #1 square in half diagonally and finger-press. Using this crease as your placement line, position a stem, a starflower, and two matching brown print diamond leaves in place. Glue baste in place on the block. Hand or machine appliqué a light brown circle B in place on the center of each flower and then a brown circle A. Make 10 of these Starflower blocks.

Make 10.

Assembled by Susan Armington; quilted by Darlene Jewell-Walhood
Finished Quilt: 88" x 88"
Finished Block: 8¾" x 8¾"

3. Repeat step 2 using the 9¼" cream print #2 squares, the remaining stems, starflowers, and light-brown print diamond leaves. Use a brown circle B and a light-brown circle A for the flower centers. Make 10 Starflower blocks.

Make 10.

4. Sew together two Starflower blocks from step 2 and two from step 3, pressing as shown by the arrows. Hand or machine appliqué a blue print #6 circle C and a brown print #1 circle B in place on the center of the blocks. The four-block section should measure 18" x 18".

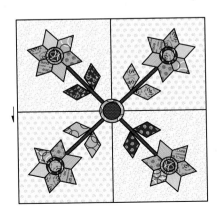

Quilt-Top Assembly

1. Arrange the Log Cabin blocks and Starflower blocks together in sections as shown, alternating the two Log Cabin blocks and rotating them to create the pattern. Sew the blocks into sections, and press in the direction of the arrows.
2. Stitch the sections together. Press.

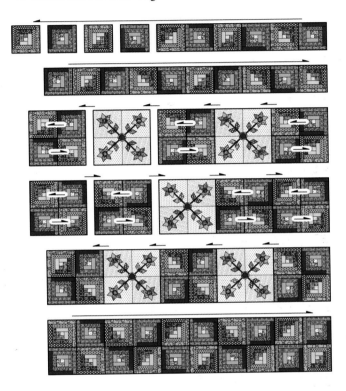

Finishing

Refer to page 12 for details on marking, layering, basting, and quilting your project. Then use the 2"-wide brown-print strips to bind the quilt.

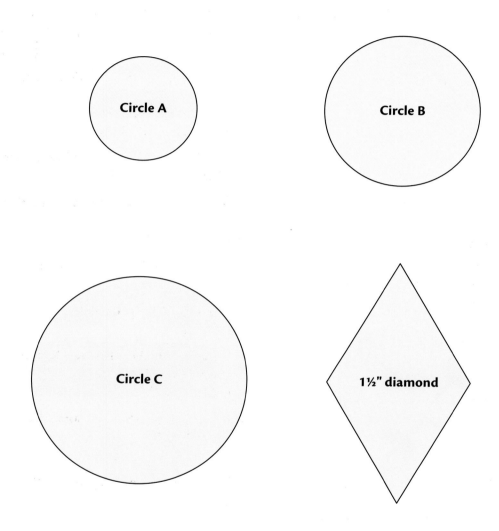

Circle A

Circle B

Circle C

1½" diamond

Stem

Diamonds and Sapphires

Diamonds can be intimidating when you're machine piecing, but that's not the case with English paper piecing! If you look closely, you'll see that each large diamond in this project is made of nine smaller diamonds. The blue-paisley fabric was my inspiration for this quilt, but it just didn't seem to be complete until I added circles to join the diamonds.

Materials

Yardage is based on 42"-wide fabric.

1¾ yards of light print for blocks

1⅜ yards of large-scale blue paisley for outer border

¾ yard of diagonally striped fabric for inner border and binding

½ yard of dark-blue tone-on-tone fabric for middle border and circles

⅜ yard *each* of 6 assorted blue prints for diamonds (2 dark blue, 2 medium blue, 1 light multi-blue, and 1 light blue)

3⅓ yards of fabric for backing

56" x 76" piece of batting

97 paper 6-point diamonds, 3"

Size 8 or 9 Sharp needle and thread to match fabric

Appliqué glue

Cutting

Refer to "English Paper Piecing 101" on page 5 for cutting diamonds; baste all diamonds to the papers. Baste the circles to papers or refer to "Freezer-Paper Appliqué" on page 9. Patterns are on page 48.

From the light print, cut:
- 9 rectangles, 11⅝" x 18⅛"

From *each* of the assorted dark-blue prints, cut:
- 20 diamonds* (40 total)

From *each* of the assorted medium-blue prints, cut:
- 16 diamonds (32)

From the light multi-blue print, cut:
- 13 diamonds

From the light-blue print, cut:
- 12 diamonds

From the diagonally striped fabric, cut:
- 5 strips, 1½" x 42"
- 7 strips, 2" x 42"

From the dark-blue tone-on-tone, cut:
- 5 strips, 2" x 42"
- 12 circles

From the large-scale blue paisley, cut:
- 6 strips, 6½" x 42"

*In the project shown, one of the dark-blue prints used in Diamond A was fussy cut to show off an elegant design, but that is optional and would depend on your fabric choices.

Making the Diamond Blocks

1. For Diamond A, whipstitch together four of each of the two dark-blue-print diamonds and a light multi-blue-print diamond as shown. Press well, remove the basting threads, and pop out the paper pieces. Make five.

Diamond A.
Make 5.

2. For Diamond B, repeat step 1 using four of each of the two medium-blue-print diamonds and one light-blue-print diamond. Make four.

Diamond B.
Make 4.

3. Center each of the diamond units onto a light-print 11⅝" x 18⅛" rectangle and glue baste in place. Hand or machine appliqué to the block.

Quilt-Top Assembly

1. Alternating Diamond A and B blocks, arrange the blocks as shown. Sew the blocks into rows, and then sew the rows together, pressing in the direction of the arrows.

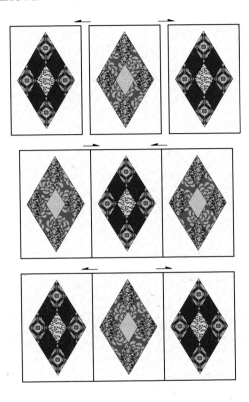

2. Whipstitch together two of each of the light multi-blue print and light-blue-print diamonds as shown. Make four. Press well, remove the basting threads, and pop out the paper pieces.

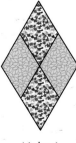

Make 4.

Quilted by Veronica Nurmi
Finished Quilt: 50⅞" x 70⅜"
Finished Block: 11⅛" x 17⅝"

3. Center each of the diamond units from step 2 onto the quilt top, aligning the diamond points with the seams. Glue baste in place and hand or machine appliqué to the quilt.

4. Center the circles between the diamond blocks as shown and appliqué in place.

Adding the Borders

1. Measure the width of the quilt through the center and cut two striped 1½" x 42" strips to that measurement for the top and bottom of the quilt. Sew to the quilt and press toward the border. Sew the three remaining striped strips together end to end at a 45° angle, measure the length of the quilt, and cut two pieces to that measurement. Sew to each side of the quilt. Press.

2. Repeat step 1 using the dark-blue tone-on-tone 2"-wide strips. Sew them to the quilt and press toward the dark-blue border.

3. Repeat the procedure for the outer border using the blue-paisley strips.

Finishing

Refer to page 12 for details on marking, layering, basting, and quilting your project. Then use the striped 2"-wide strips to bind the quilt.

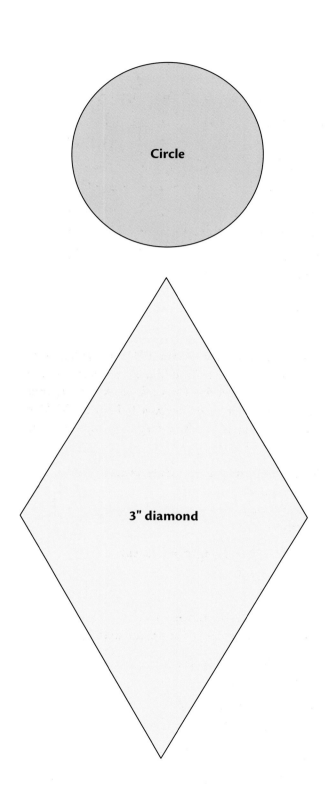

Circle

3" diamond

Just Judie

I'm always drawn to scrappy quilts, but I seem to have a hard time designing them. After collecting Judie Rothermel's Civil War reproduction fabrics for years (Judie is my friend and a very talented designer), I made up my mind to try a scrappy quilt that would use only a very small portion of each fabric, so I would have plenty left for another project. I decided to try the "paper-bag method." I would put all of my basted hexagons into a bag, and then pull them out one by one as the next to be sewn to the quilt. But first I separated my hexagons into color groups and put each color in a separate bag. That was much better. Did I mention I used clear plastic bags? I guess it's a control issue! Regardless, I was happy with the result, which is the important thing. This quilt is a tribute to my friend Judie.

Materials

Yardage is based on 42"-wide fabric, unless otherwise noted. Precut 5" charm squares would be a perfect fit for the diamonds and hexagons in this project.

4¼ yards *total* of assorted dark prints for hexagons and border appliqués (or 234 dark 5" charm squares)

1½ yards *total* of assorted light prints for diamonds and triangles (or 85 light 5" charm squares)

⅞ yard of light print #1 for side borders

¾ yard of dark-green print for vines in border

⅔ yard of light print #2 for top and bottom borders

⅝ yard of fabric for binding

3⅓ yards of fabric for backing

58" x 77" piece of batting

187 paper hexagons, 2"

254 paper 6-point diamonds, 2"

20 paper equilateral triangles, 2"

Size 8 or 9 Sharp needle and thread to blend with fabric

Appliqué glue

Wave Edge Ruler (optional)

Cutting

Refer to "English Paper Piecing 101" on page 5 for cutting hexagons, diamonds, and triangles; baste all the shapes to the papers. Baste the circles to papers or refer to "Freezer-Paper Appliqué" on page 9. Refer to "Making Bias Vines" on page 11 for cutting bias strips. Patterns are on page 54.

From the assorted dark prints, cut:
- 187 hexagons
- 94 diamonds
- 4 circles

From the assorted light prints, cut:
- 160 diamonds
- 20 triangles

From the dark-green print, cut:
- 1¼" bias strips to total approximately 260"

From light print #2, cut:
- 2 strips, 7" x 42"

From light print #1, cut:
- 4 strips, 7" x 42"

From the binding fabric, cut:
- 7 strips, 2" x 42"

Making the Quilt

1. Whipstitch together 17 assorted hexagons to make one vertical row.

2. The next vertical row will begin with an assorted light triangle, followed by 16 assorted light diamonds and ending with an assorted light triangle. Whipstitch each of these to the hexagon row from step 1 as shown.

3. Continue adding hexagon rows and diamond rows until there are 10 of each. You can add the hexagons individually, or sew them into rows first. Stitch one more row of hexagons to the right end. The basting and paper pieces can be removed as you add rows. However, be sure to leave the papers in the top and bottom pieces and in the side rows until the entire quilt center is finished and the sides are trimmed.

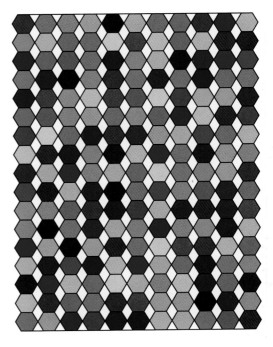

4. Trim the sides of the quilt ¼" beyond the center of the first and last hexagon rows as shown. Remove any remaining paper pieces. The quilt should now measure approximately 40½" x 59½".

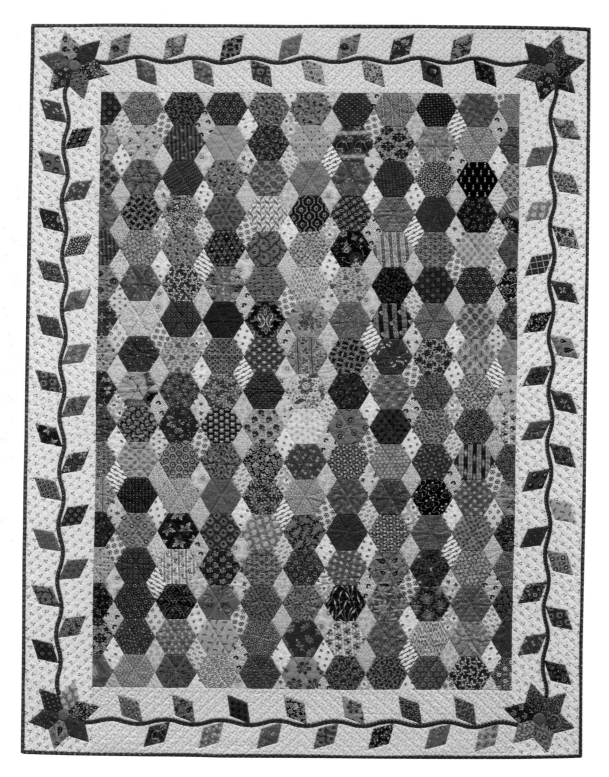

Quilted by Vicki Bellino
Finished Quilt: 53½" x 72½"

Adding the Border

Measure your quilt before cutting the borders and make adjustments as needed.

1. Cut two 7" x 40½" strips from the light print #2 strips for the top and bottom borders. Using a water-soluble marking pen and a Wave Edge Ruler (or the wave pattern provided on page 54), draw a curved line down the center of the strip. With the vine extending 4" from the end of the border, apply a few drops of appliqué glue to the wrong side of the vine and glue baste onto the curved line as you move down the border. Leave approximately 4" of vine free at the ends of each border strip and extending 4" off the end of the border strip.

2. Evenly space 14 assorted dark-print diamonds down the vine and machine or hand appliqué in place. Make two of these border strips and sew to the top and bottom of the quilt.

3. Piece two 7" x 42" light print #1 strips together and cut to 72½" long. Make two for the side borders.

4. Repeat steps 1 and 2 using the 7" x 72½" light print #1 strips. For the side borders, do not include the extra 4" of vine. Evenly space 21 assorted dark-print diamonds on each side-border strip, glue baste in place, and hand or machine appliqué to the border. Sew a strip to each side of the quilt.

5. Whipstitch together six assorted dark diamonds to make one starflower. Press well, remove the basting, and pop out the paper pieces. Make four flowers.

Make 4.

6. Place a starflower on each corner of the quilt. Continue curving the vine to 1" beyond and under the starflower and glue baste in place. Hand or machine appliqué to the quilt. Center a dark-print circle onto each flower and appliqué in place.

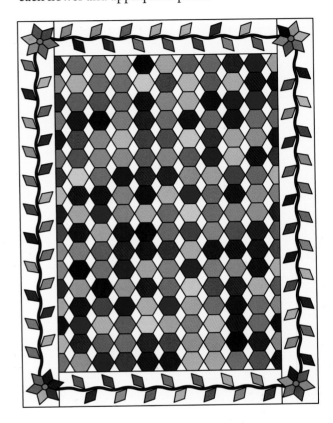

Finishing

Refer to page 12 for details on marking, layering, basting, and quilting your project. Then use the 2"-wide strips to bind the quilt.

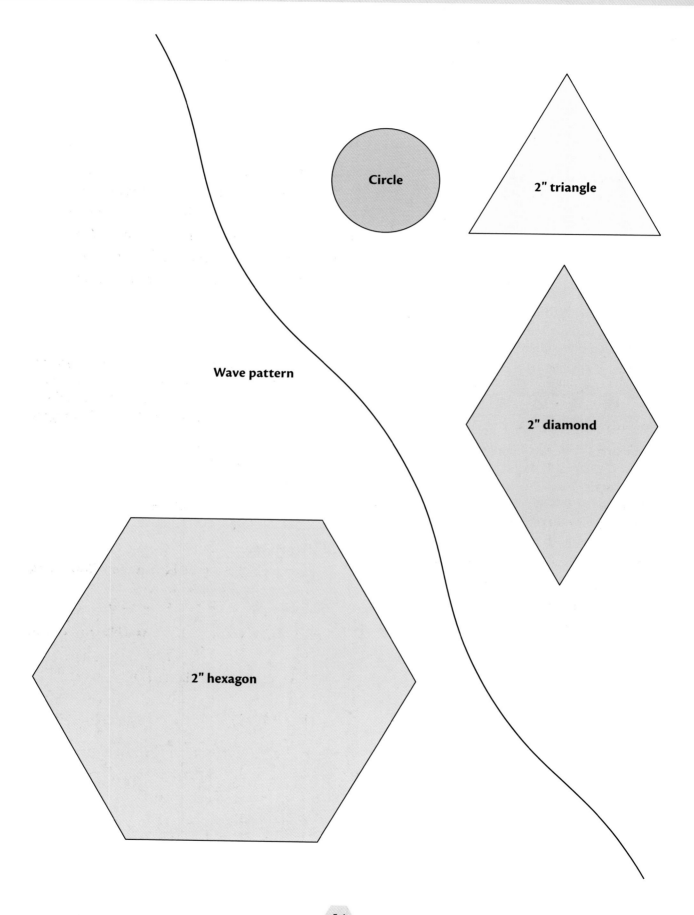

Circle

2" triangle

2" diamond

Wave pattern

2" hexagon

A Dresden Delight

Finished Quilt: 16" x 16"

I often find that small projects fill that need for instant gratification, giving me a break from a huge endeavor that takes forever to complete. After painting our kitchen and dining-room walls a deep red, I decided to frame a small project that would enhance the Provençal colors I love so much. This project could easily be quilted and bound for a beautiful table topper or wall hanging, but instructions are provided for framing. I purchased a ready-made frame and had a local art store frame the project with nonglare, museum-quality glass.

Materials

Yardage is based on 42"-wide fabric unless otherwise specified. This project is perfect for charm squares, as two Dresden plate pieces will fit nicely onto a 5" square.

½ yard of cream pindot fabric for block background

1 fat eighth of red pindot fabric for scalloped border and center circle

10" square of blue pindot fabric for circles

5" x 10" piece *each* of 2 red, 2 yellow, 2 blue, and 2 green prints* for Dresden Plate

18" x 18" piece of batting

16 Chrysanthemum paper pieces, $1\frac{1}{16}$" x $3\frac{11}{16}$"

16 Dresden paper pieces, $3\frac{11}{16}$"

Picture frame with 16" x 16" opening

*Or you can use 4 charm squares (5" x 5") each of the 4 assorted colors.

Cutting

Refer to "English Paper Piecing 101" on page 5 for cutting the Dresden plate and Chrysanthemum pieces; baste all the shapes to the papers. Baste the circles to papers or refer to "Freezer-Paper Appliqué" on page 9. Patterns are on page 58.

From the cream pindot fabric, cut:
- 1 square, 17" x 17"

From the red pindot fabric, cut:
- 4 scalloped edge A
- 1 circle C

From *each* of the assorted green and yellow prints, cut:
- 4 Chrysanthemum pieces (16 total)

From *each* of the assorted red and blue prints, cut:
- 4 Dresden pieces (16 total)

From the blue pindot fabric, cut:
- 1 circle B
- 4 partial circle B

Making the Dresden Plate

1. Alternating red, yellow, blue, and green Dresden and Chrysanthemum pieces, whipstitch 16 together to form the Dresden Plate. Press well on both sides, remove the basting, and pop out the paper pieces.

2. From the remaining Dresden and Chrysanthemum pieces, whipstitch four together—one from each color group. Make four of these partial Dresden Plates for the corners.

Assembly

1. Center the Dresden Plate onto the 17" cream square and glue baste in place. Hand or machine appliqué to the block.
2. Center and appliqué circle B in place, followed by circle C.

3. Center a scallop A in place on the top and bottom of the block and glue baste (or fuse) in place. Hand or machine appliqué to the block. Repeat for each side.

4. Place a partial Dresden Plate in each corner of the block, overlapping the ends of each scalloped edge, and appliqué in place.
5. Place a partial circle B onto each corner and appliqué in place.

Finishing

Mark the block for quilting, baste to an 18" x 18" piece of batting, and quilt the project as desired. It's now ready for framing.

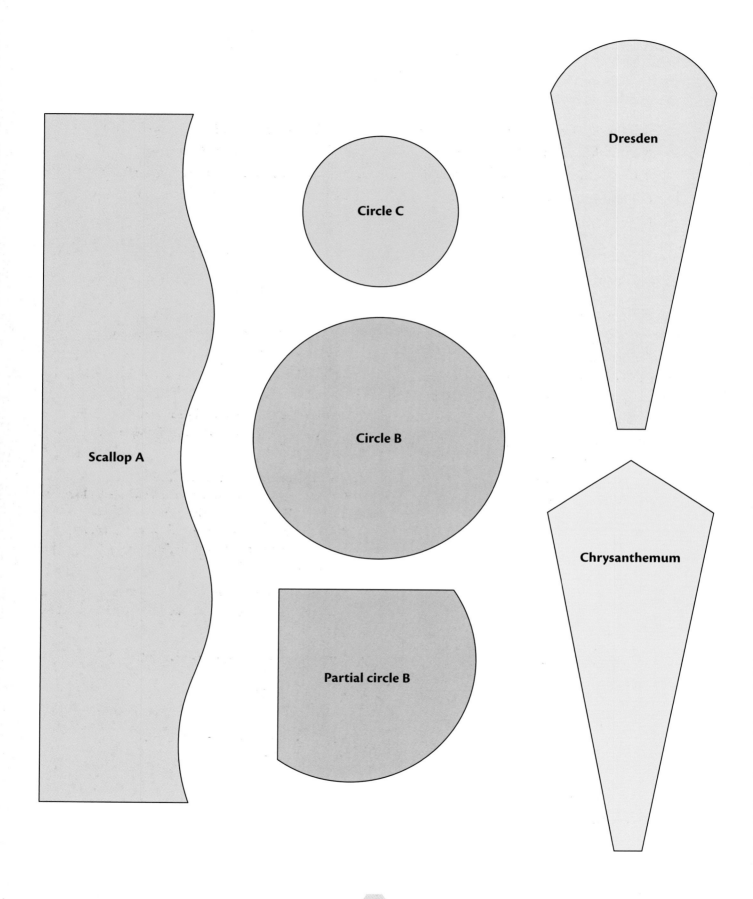

Scallop A

Circle C

Circle B

Partial circle B

Dresden

Chrysanthemum

Dresdens on the Vine

Miniature Dresden Plates are so adorable. I've used them on small doll quilts, appliquéd them onto little girls' dresses, and couldn't resist them on the vine in this project! For a cheery and bright table runner or wall hanging, I chose an assortment of 1930s reproduction prints. Precut 5" charm squares would also work well for the blocks, flowers, and leaves.

Materials

Yardage is based on 42"-wide fabric.

⅝ yard of small-scale light print for appliqué background and setting triangles

½ yard of small-scale green print for leaves, inner border, and binding

⅓ yard of large-scale floral print for outer border

1 fat quarter of green solid for bias vine and leaves

1 fat quarter of light multicolored print for blocks

1 fat eighth *each* of 2 red, 2 blue, and 2 yellow prints for Dresden petals and circles

1½ yards of fabric for backing

24" x 50" piece of batting

48 miniature Dresden paper pieces, ¹³⁄₁₆"

Size 8 or 9 Sharp needle and thread to match fabric

Appliqué glue

Cutting

Refer to "English Paper Piecing 101" on page 5 for cutting the Dresden petals; baste all the shapes to the papers. Baste the circles and leaves to papers or refer to "Freezer-Paper Appliqué" on page 9. Patterns are on page 63. Refer to "Making Bias Vines" on page 11 for cutting bias strips.

From *each* of the 2 red prints and 1 yellow print, cut:
- 8 Dresden petals (24 total)
- 4 squares, 2½" x 2½" (12 total)
- 1 flower center (3 total)

From the second yellow print, cut:
- 8 Dresden petals
- 8 squares, 2½" x 2½"
- 1 flower center

From *each* of the assorted blue fabrics, cut:
- 8 Dresden petals (16 total)
- 1 flower center (2 total)
- 6 squares, 2½" x 2½" (12 total)

From the light multicolored print, cut:
- 4 strips, 2½" x 21"; crosscut into 28 squares, 2½" x 2½"

From the small-scale light print, cut:
- 6 squares, 7" x 7"; cut into quarters diagonally for a total of 24 side setting triangles
- 4 squares, 3¾" x 3¾"; cut in half diagonally for a total of 8 corner setting triangles
- 1 strip, 3½" x 40¾"

From the green solid, cut:
- 1¼"-wide bias strips to total 45"
- 7 leaves

From the small-scale green print, cut:
- 3 strips, 1" x 42"
- 4 strips, 2" x 42"
- 7 leaves

From the large-scale floral print, cut:
- 3 strips, 2½" x 42"

Making the Four-Patch Block Rows

1. With right sides together, sew a 2½" light multicolored-print square to each of the 2½" assorted red, blue, and yellow squares, pressing away from the multicolored print. Sew a Four Patch block using two units from the same color group. Make four red, four yellow, and six blue blocks.

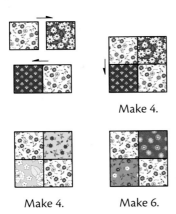

Make 4.

Make 4.   Make 6.

2. For each vertical Four Patch row, sew together seven Four Patch blocks, 12 side setting triangles, and four corner setting triangles as shown. Note that the top and bottom blocks are oriented so that the colored squares are horizontal. Press the seam allowances toward the triangles in each row; press the seam allowances in one direction after sewing the rows together.

Make 2.

3. Repeat step 2 for the second row, rotating the five Four Patch blocks in the center of the row 180° so that the print squares will be in different positions in the second row.

Making the Dresden Flower Row

1. Whipstitch together eight Dresden petals from the same color group. Make six Dresden flowers. Press well, remove the basting thread, and gently pop out the paper pieces.

Make 2 of each.

2. Sew a Four Patch block row to each side of the 3½" x 40¾" light small-scale print strip. Press seam allowances toward the center strip. Trim the center strip, if necessary, so that it's the same length as the block rows.

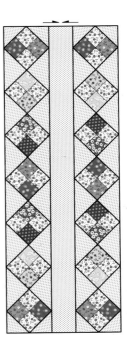

3. Gently curve the bias vine down the center of the 3½"-wide strip and glue baste as you move down the strip. Arrange the Dresden flowers and leaves down the vine and glue baste in place. Hand or machine

Quilted by Veronica Nurmi
Finished Quilt: 19⅞" x 45⅛"

appliqué the vine, leaves, and flowers to the strip. Place a center circle on each of the flowers and appliqué in place.

Quilt-Top Assembly

1. Measure your quilt horizontally through the center. From the 1" x 42" small-scale green-print strips, crosscut two pieces to that length and sew them to the top and bottom of the quilt, pressing toward the green print.
2. Measure the quilt vertically through the center and cut two green strips to that length. Sew them to the sides of the quilt and press toward the green strips.
3. Measure the quilt horizontally and vertically through the center and cut four border strips from the 2½" x 42" floral strips. Sew the top and bottom borders to the quilt.

4. Sew a 2½" yellow square to each end of the side border strips; press toward the border strips. Sew to each side of the quilt and press.

Finishing

Refer to page 12 for details on marking, layering, basting, and quilting your project. Then use the 2"-wide small-scale green-print strips to bind the quilt.

Simply Stated

Here's another example of keeping a design simple. This quilt provides an opportunity to showcase unique and exquisite appliqué as well as beautiful quilting. I chose a limited color palette, but I could also see this as a much scrappier quilt. With the muslin background, this would make a wonderful wedding gift.

Materials

Yardage is based on 42"-wide fabric.

6½ yards of muslin for Square blocks, side and corner triangles, outer border, and binding

¾ yard of tan print for stems and leaves

⅔ yard of red-and-blue print for Square blocks and inner border

⅜ yard of red tone-on-tone print for Flower blocks

⅜ yard of blue tone-on-tone print for Flower blocks

5 yards of fabric for backing

74" x 89" piece of batting

48 Chrysanthemum paper pieces, $1\frac{1}{16}$" x $3\frac{11}{16}$"

Size 8 or 9 Sharp needle and thread to match fabric

Appliqué glue and freezer paper

OR 1¾ yards of 18"-wide lightweight fusible web for fusible appliqué

Cutting

To minimize the number of seams, the red-and-blue print squares were appliquéd onto the muslin squares in the project shown. You may machine piece these blocks, if you prefer, referring to the asterisked note for alternate cutting. Refer to "English Paper Piecing 101" on page 5 for cutting Chrysanthemum pieces; baste all the shapes to the papers. Refer to "Freezer-Paper Appliqué" on page 9 to prepare the squares, stems, and leaves. Patterns are on pages 68 and 69.

From the muslin, cut:
- 4 squares, 15½" x 15½"; cut into quarters diagonally for a total of 16 triangles (2 are extra)
- 32 squares, 10½" x 10½"*
- 2 squares, 8" x 8"; cut in half diagonally for a total of 4 corner triangles
- 8 strips, 6½" x 42"
- 8 strips, 2" x 42"

From *each* of the red and blue tone-on-tone prints, cut:
- 24 Chrysanthemum pieces (48 total)

From the red-and-blue print, cut:
- 20 squares, 4½" x 4½"**
- 7 strips, 1" x 42"

From the tan print, cut:
- 12 stems
- 12 leaves and 12 leaves reversed

*To machine piece the 20 setting blocks, cut 40 rectangles, 3½" x 4½", and 40 rectangles, 3½" x 10½". Cut just 12 squares, 10½" x 10½", for the flower blocks.

**Cut 20 squares, 4" x 4", of freezer paper for freezer-paper appliqué. For fusible appliqué, draw 4" x 4" squares on the paper side of fusible web and fuse to the wrong side of the red-and-blue print fabric.

Quilted by Vicki Bellino
Finished Quilt: 70" x 84¼"
Finished Block: 10" x 10"

Making the Square Blocks

For appliqué: Fold 20 of the 10½" muslin squares in half diagonally in each direction and press a crease to find the center. Center a prepared red-and-blue print square onto each of the squares. Hand or machine appliqué in place.

Make 20.

For machine piecing: Sew a 3½" x 4½" muslin rectangle to the top and bottom of each of the 4½" red-and-blue print squares; press toward the muslin. Sew a 3½" x 10½" muslin rectangle to each side. Press. Make 20 blocks.

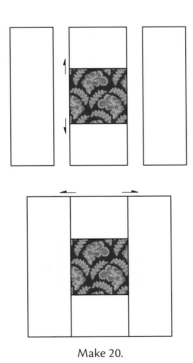

Make 20.

Making the Flower Blocks

1. Alternating two red and two blue Chrysanthemum petals, whipstitch four together for each flower. Make 12. Press well, remove the basting, and pop out the paper pieces.
2. Using the Flower block placement guide on page 69, position a flower, stem, and leaves onto a 10½" muslin square. Hand or machine appliqué in place. Make 12.

Make 12.

Quilt-Top Assembly

1. Arrange the Flower blocks and Square blocks together in diagonal rows as shown. Add the side and corner setting triangles. Sew the blocks into diagonal rows, pressing toward the setting triangles and Flower blocks. Add the corner triangles last.

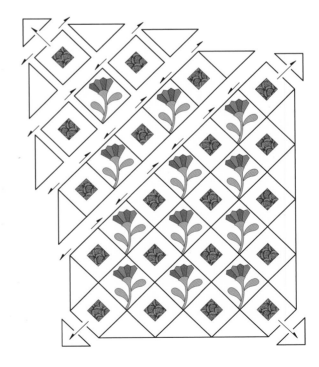

2. Sew the 1"-wide red-and-blue print strips together end to end at a 45° angle. Measure the width of the quilt through the center and cut two pieces to that length for the top and bottom of the quilt. Sew to the quilt, pressing toward the print. Repeat for the side borders using the remaining 1"-wide red-and-blue print strips.

3. Repeat step 2 using the 6½"-wide muslin strips.

Finishing

Refer to page 12 for details on marking, layering, basting, and quilting your project. Then use the 2"-wide muslin strips to bind the quilt.

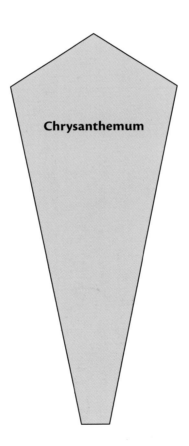

Chrysanthemum

Flower block placement guide

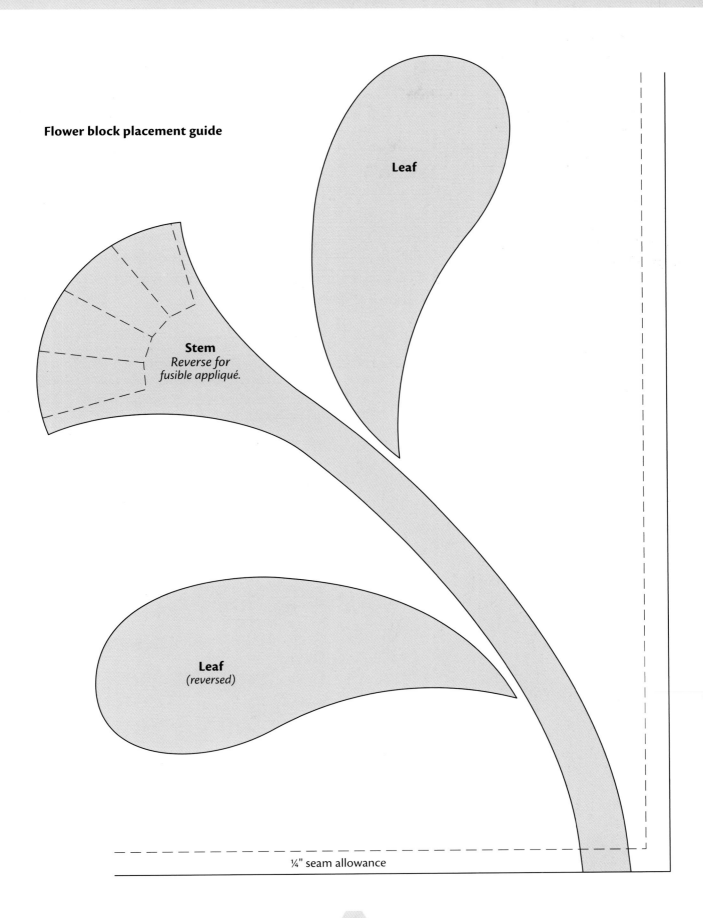

Leaf

Stem
*Reverse for
fusible appliqué.*

Leaf
(reversed)

¼" seam allowance

Dresdens Defined

I'm always on the lookout for innovative ways to use English paper piecing, and when I was given the opportunity to design with Strip-It, a printed fabric designed to look like a sewn strip set, I immediately thought of using Dresden blade paper pieces. This fabric, from the Definitions line by Marcus Fabrics, has 17 stripes of assorted prints across the fabric width. The illusion is that there are 32 sections to this Dresden Plate, but there are really only 16. The trick is using the Strip-It and the placement of your paper piece when you cut out the blades. While this particular fabric may no longer be available, there will be new Strip-It prints on the market each season.

Materials

1 yard of Strip-It for Dresden Plates*

1 yard of solid-black fabric for Dresden blocks, Square-in-a-Square blocks, and binding

⅞ yard of brown floral for sashing

½ yard of light-gray print for Dresden blocks

½ yard of light-tan print for Dresden blocks

½ yard of gray print for Square-in-a-Square blocks

3 yards of fabric for backing

48" x 48" piece of batting

64 Dresden blade paper pieces (Chrysanthemum, 1¹⁄₁₆" x 3¹¹⁄₁₆")

Size 8 or 9 Sharp needle and thread to match fabric

Appliqué glue

Or 17 assorted strips, 2½" x 42"

Cutting

Refer to "English Paper Piecing 101" on page 5 for cutting Dresden blades; baste all the shapes to the papers. Baste the circles to papers or refer to "Freezer-Paper Appliqué" on page 9. Patterns are on page 74.

From *each* of the light-gray and light-tan prints, cut:
- 2 squares, 12½" x 12½" (4 total)

From the brown floral, cut:
- 2 strips, 13½" x 42"; crosscut into 12 rectangles, 6½" x 13½"

From the solid-black fabric, cut:
- 6 strips, 1" x 42"; crosscut into:
  8 strips, 1" x 12½"
  8 strips, 1" x 13½"
- 4 strips, 3½" x 42"; crosscut 36 squares, 3½" x 3½"
- 5 strips, 2" x 42"
- 4 circles

From the gray print, cut:
- 2 strips, 6½" x 42"; crosscut 9 squares, 6½" x 6½"

Quilted by Veronica Nurmi
Finished Quilt: 44½" x 44½"
Finished Block: 12" x 12"

Cutting the Dresden Plate Pieces

If you're using Strip-It fabric, place the paper piece on the fabric as shown, placing the point along the line where two stripes meet, and centering the lower edge along the stripe. Cut 64.

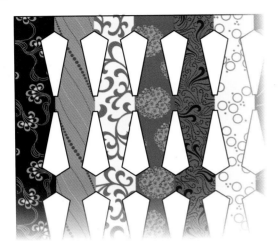

If you're using 2½" x 42" strips of fabric, sew them together in groups of two or three, using a shorter-than-normal stitch length. Press the seam allowances open. Cut the 64 Dresden pieces in the same way as shown for the Strip-It fabric above.

Making the Dresden Plate Blocks

1. Whipstitch together 16 assorted Dresden blades on the long sides. Press well on both sides, remove the basting, and pop out the paper pieces. Make four Dresden Plates.
2. Center a Dresden Plate onto each 12½" light-gray and light-tan square and glue baste in place. Hand or machine appliqué to the squares. Center a solid-black circle onto each Dresden plate and appliqué in place. Make four blocks.

3. Sew a 1" x 12½" solid-black strip to the top and bottom of each block from step 2, pressing toward the black fabric. Sew a 1" x 13½" solid-black strip to each side. Press.

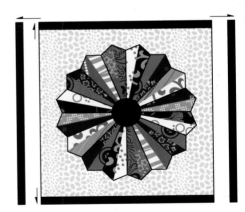

Making the Square-in-a-Square Blocks

Draw a diagonal line with a white marking pencil on the wrong side of each 3½" solid-black square. With right sides together, lay one of these squares onto a corner of each 6½" gray-print square. Sew on the drawn line; trim the seam allowances to ¼" and press toward the corner. Repeat these steps for the remaining corners. Make nine of these blocks.

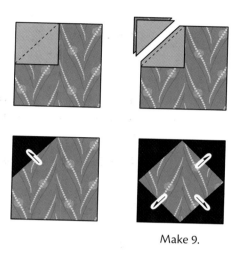

Make 9.

Quilt-Top Assembly

Sew the Dresden Plate blocks, Square-in-a-Square blocks, and 6½" x 13½" brown floral sashing rectangles together as shown, pressing in the direction of the arrows.

Finishing

Refer to page 12 for details on marking, layering, basting, and quilting your project. Then use the 2"-wide solid-black strips to bind the quilt.

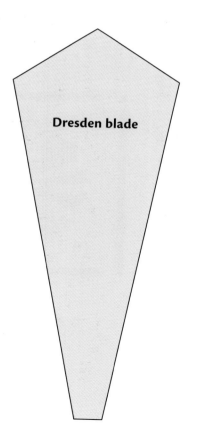

Dresden blade

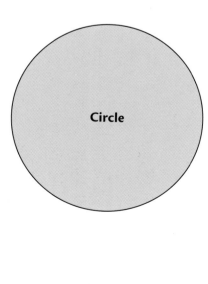

Circle

Pentarings for Baby

I'd never used pentagons in English paper piecing until I began playing around with this design for the book. I quickly realized that pentagon shapes are fun and quick to baste, and they make the cutest rings when whipstitched together. For this quilt I chose fabrics suitable for either a baby boy or a baby girl, but I could picture it done in all blues or all pinks too. With easy appliqué and simple blocks, you'll have this project done in no time!

Materials

Yardage is based on 42"-wide fabric.

1 yard of large-scale light print for center rectangle and outer border

½ yard *each* of 2 light prints (polka dots and rickrack) for blocks and border corner squares

½ yard of solid-blue fabric for inner border and binding

1 fat eighth *each* of assorted small-scale prints for pentagon rings (red, green, brown, blue, and peach)

1⅛ yards of fabric for backing

35" x 42" piece of batting

100 pentagon paper pieces, 1"

Size 8 or 9 Sharp needle and thread to match fabric

Appliqué glue

Cutting

Refer to "English Paper Piecing 101" on page 5 for cutting pentagons; baste all the pentagons to the papers. The pentagon pattern is on page 79.

From *each* of the assorted small-scale prints, cut:
- 20 pentagons (100 total)

From *each* of the polka-dot and rickrack light prints, cut:
- 2 squares, 4½" x 4½" (4 total)
- 2 strips, 4" x 42" (4 total)

From the large-scale light print, cut:
- 4 strips, 4½" x 42"; crosscut into:
  2 pieces, 4½" x 22½"
  2 pieces, 4½" x 29½"
- 1 rectangle, 6½" x 13½"

From the solid-blue fabric, cut:
- 6 strips, 1" x 42"; crosscut into:
  2 pieces, 1" x 6½"
  2 pieces, 1" x 14½"
  2 pieces, 1" x 21½"
  2 pieces, 1" x 29½"
- 4 strips, 2" x 42"

Making the Blocks

1. With right sides together, sew a 4"-wide polka-dot strip to a rickrack strip; press toward the rickrack. Make two strip sets. Crosscut 4"-wide segments for a total of 20 units, 4" x 7½" each.

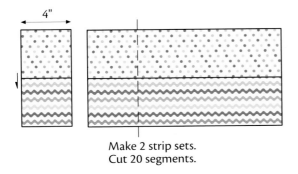

Make 2 strip sets.
Cut 20 segments.

2. Sew together two of the units from step 1 to make a Four Patch block, 7½" x 7½". Make 10 blocks.

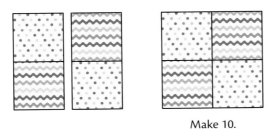

Make 10.

3. Each pentagon ring will consist of two pentagons from each color group. Alternating the five assorted prints, whipstitch 10 together to form a ring. Make 10. Press well on both sides, remove the basting, and pop out the paper pieces.

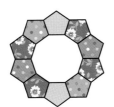

Make 10.

4. Center each pentagon ring onto a Four Patch block and glue baste in place. Hand or machine appliqué to the block.

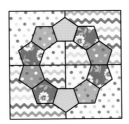

Quilt-Top Assembly

1. With right sides together, sew 1" x 6½" blue strips to the top and bottom of the 6½" x 13½" large-scale light-print rectangle, pressing toward the blue fabric. Sew a 1" x 14½" blue strip to each side. Press.

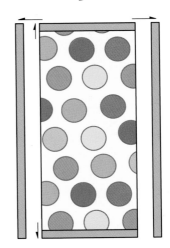

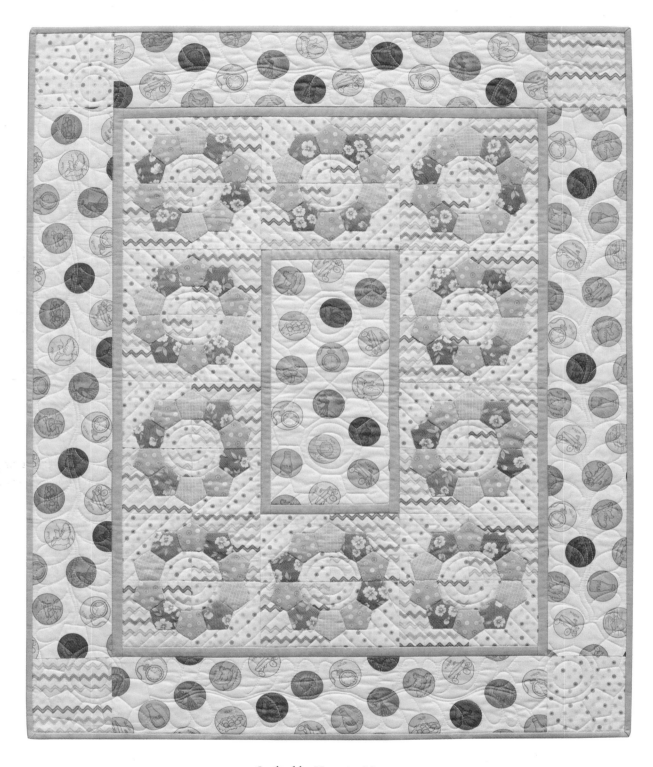

Quilted by Veronica Nurmi
Finished Quilt: 30½" x 37½"
Finished Block: 7" x 7"

2. Sew the blocks around the rectangle from step 1, pressing as shown by the arrows.

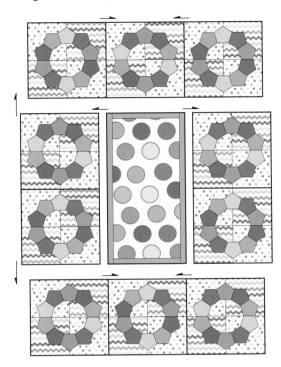

3. Sew 1" x 21½" blue strips to the top and bottom of the quilt. Press toward blue strips. Sew a 1" x 29½" blue strip to each side. Press.

4. Sew 4½" x 22½" large-scale light-print strips to the top and bottom of the quilt and press toward the light print. Sew a 4½" polka-dot square to one end of each of the 4½" x 29½" large-scale light-print strips;

press toward the large-scale print. Repeat, sewing the 4½" rickrack squares to the remaining ends. Sew one of these borders to each side of the quilt. Press toward the just-added border.

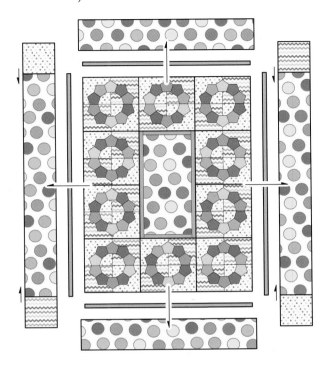

Finishing

Refer to page 12 for details on marking, layering, basting, and quilting your project. Then use the 2"-wide solid-blue strips to bind the quilt.

1" pentagon

Acknowledgments

I couldn't write a book about English paper piecing without expressing my gratitude to JoAnn Lewis, owner of Paper Pieces, for her generosity, support, and never-ending enthusiasm for English paper piecing.

To Susan Armington, Veronica Nurmi, and Darlene Walhood for being my "right-hand women" when it came to making and quilting several of the projects in this book. I couldn't have accomplished all of this without you!

My thanks to Moda for providing me with an assortment of beautiful fat-quarter bundles for some of the projects in this book.

To my wonderful husband for his patience, encouragement, love, and support. I'm so lucky to have him by my side.

And last, but certainly not least, to all of my friends at Marcus Fabrics for their boundless support, their generosity, and most importantly, their friendship.

About the Author

Vicki Bellino makes her home in far northern California, in a city known for its extreme summer heat as well as beautiful rivers, lakes, and mountains. She and her husband enjoy spending their free time in the outdoors, and with their four beautiful granddaughters, Madilyn, Lexi, Ava, and Olyvia.

Vicki learned to quilt in 1986 and hasn't stopped since! She was introduced to English paper piecing (or EPP as she calls it) a few years ago and instantly became enamored with the technique.

Vicki's had the opportunity to teach EPP at many quilt shops, as well as to anyone interested in learning. She taught her two oldest granddaughters, and Lexi (age 11) has since become an avid and skillful paper piecer. In fact, Lexi and Vicki hope to design a few projects together in the near future.

Vicki strongly believes in personal choices regarding quiltmaking techniques and materials. She would be remiss, however, if she didn't mention that the best choice she has ever made was to marry her high-school sweetheart, Dante, now her husband of 38 years. His never-ending support, encouragement, and patience have afforded her the opportunity to be the crazy, creative, and compulsive quilter she is today!

There's More Online!

Read Vicki's blog, shop her latest patterns, and sign the guest book at www.bloomcreek.com. Order paper pieces at www.paperpieces.com. And find more great books on quilting at www.martingale-pub.com.